EXPRESS EDITION

On the Front Line

SURVIVING THE HOLOCAUST

Cath Senker

Chicago, Illinois

Produced for Raintree Publishers by Discovery Books Ltd
Editorial: Kathryn Walker, Juliet Smith, and Daniel Nunn
Design: Rob Norridge, Michelle Lisseter, and Clare
  Nicholas
Expert reader: David Downing
Picture research: Elaine Fuoco-Lang
Project manager: Juliet Smith
Production: Duncan Gilbert
Printed and bound in China by South China Printing
  Company Ltd
Originated by Dot Gradations Ltd

10 09 08 07 06
10 9 8 7 6 5 4 3 2 1

Library of Congress Cataloging-in-Publication Data
Senker, Cath.
  Surviving the Holocaust / Cath Senker.
    p. cm. -- (Freestyle express) (On the front line)
  Includes bibliographical references and index.
  ISBN 1-4109-2197-2 (lib. bindg.) -- ISBN 1-4109-2204-9
  (pbk.) 1. Holocaust, Jewish (1939-1945)--Juvenile
  literature. 2. Holocaust, Jewish (1939-1945)--Biography--
  Juvenile literature. I. Title. II. Series. III. Series: On the
  front line

D804.34.S464 2006
940.53'18--dc22

                                              2005027092

This leveled text is a version of *Freestyle:
On the Front Line: Surviving the Holocaust*

Original edition produced by White-Thomson Publishing
Ltd, Bridgewater Business Centre, 210 High Street, Lewes
BN7 2NH, United Kingdom.

Acknowledgments
The publishers would like to thank the following for
permission to reproduce photographs:
AKG images pp. 4–5, 6 (l), 6–7, 7 (r), 12 (l), 12 (r),
**15, 16, 18, 19, 20, 23, 24, 25, 26–27, 29, 30, 31,
32–33, 35, 36, 41**; Corbis p. 39; Holocaust Memorial
Museum Library pp. 5 (l), 9, 10, 14; Michael Shocket
p. 14 (l); Popperfoto pp. 17, 37; Topfoto pp. 8, 11,
19 (r), **21, 22, 24** (l), **27** (r), **28, 28** (l), **32** (l), **34, 38,
40** (l); Zvi Kadushin/Beth Hatefutsoth, Nahum Goldmann
Museum of Jewish Diaspora p. 18 (l).

Cover photograph of prisoners freed from Oswiecim in
January 1945 reproduced with permission of Topfoto.

Map on p.13 by Jillian Luff.

The publishers would like to thank the following for
permission to reproduce extracts: pp. 10–11 Story adapted
from *The Necklace* by Lee Edwards, in *I Came Alone*
edited by Bertha Leverton and Shmuel Lowensohn; p. 15
Anne Frank quote adapted from *Anne Frank: The Diary of
a Young Girl* (Puffin, 1997).

Source notes: pp. **8–9** *Never Again* by Martin Gilbert,
p. 43; pp. **10–11** *I Came Alone* edited by Bertha Leverton
and Shmuel Lowensohn, p. 403; pp. **14–15** *Know Me
Tomorrow* by Michael Shocket; pp. **16–17** *Never Again*,
p. 55; pp. **20–21** statistics from *Never Again* p. 71;
pp. **20–21** Victor Breitburg's story from Lodz
ShtetLinks http://www.shtetlinks.jewishgen.org/lodz/
holocaust.htm#Testimonies; pp. **26–27** Max Perkal from
Outside was Beautiful by Max Perkal; pp. **32–33** from
Yad Vashem, Israel; Abba Kovner quote from *Tough Jews*
by Rich Cohen; pp. **38–39** Bella's story from the Nizkor
Project; p. **41** death figures from *Introducing the Holocaust*
by Haim Bresheeth, Stuart Hood, and Litza Jansz.

Every effort has been made to contact copyright holders
of any material reproduced in this book. Any omissions
will be rectified in subsequent printings if notice is given
to the publishers.

The paper used to print this book comes from sustainable
resources.

CONTENTS

Any words appearing in the text in bold, **like this**, are explained in the glossary. You can also look out for them in the Word Bank box at the bottom of each page.

A BRITISH MAN IN AUSCHWITZ

What was the Holocaust?

Between 1933 and 1945, the National Socialist (Nazi) Party was in power in Germany. In late 1941, the Nazis decided to kill all the Jews in Europe. The Nazis also murdered **Roma** (gypsies), gay people, disabled people, and people who disagreed with them. By 1945 the Nazis had murdered about six million Jews. This mass murder of Jews is now known as the **Holocaust**.

Leon Greenman was born in Great Britain in 1910. When World War II began in 1939, Leon was in the Netherlands (a country sometimes called Holland). He lived there with his wife and young son.

Trapped

In May 1940 Germany invaded the Netherlands. The **Nazis** were at war with Britain, and they hated Jewish people. Leon was British and Jewish. He knew that he and his family were in terrible danger.

In January 1945 the Soviet army freed these prisoners from Auschwitz concentration camp in Poland.

Word Bank   Nazis people in the political party that ran Germany from 1933 to 1945

In October 1942 the Nazis put Leon and his family on a train. It took them to Auschwitz-Birkenau. Auschwitz-Birkenau was a **death camp**. This was a place where people were taken to be killed. At Auschwitz the men were separated from the women and children. Leon never saw his wife and son again.

Survival

Leon survived three years of terrible hard work in **labor camps**. These were prisons where people had to work for the Germans. Leon was one of the very few who survived Auschwitz. He now travels around talking about his experiences.

Find out later

How did some Jewish people hide from the Nazis?

Which countries helped the Jews escape?

What happened to people who survived the Holocaust?

death camp   camp where the Nazis sent Jews and others to be killed

THE NAZIS AND THE HOLOCAUST

This Nazi poster shows a healthy, blonde-haired Aryan girl. The Nazis used images like this to persuade people that pure-blooded Germans were better than anyone else.

In 1918 Germany lost World War I. It had to pay a lot of money to the countries that won the war. Germany also had to give away some of its richest land. It became a poor country. Millions of German people had no jobs.

The Nazi Party

In 1919 a political party called the National Socialist German Workers' Party, or **Nazi** Party, was set up in Germany. Adolf Hitler became its leader in 1921.

Word Bank   **Aryans**   people from Germany and Scandinavia whom the Nazis thought were superior to everyone else

Nazis thought that white-skinned northern European people were better than anyone else. They called these people **Aryans**. The Nazis blamed other people for Germany's problems. They particularly blamed Jews.

Hitler's promise

Germany's problems got worse. Hitler promised the Germans he would win back German land. He also promised to give everyone jobs. In January 1933 Hitler was asked to be the leader of Germany.

Nazi views
In 1920 the Nazis said:
"Only people of German blood can be members of our nation, whatever their religion. No Jewish person may be a member of the nation."

Hundreds of men line up outside a German factory in 1930. They are hoping to find some work.

Adolf Hitler, the leader of the German Nazi Party.

Hitler in power

In March 1933 the German parliament (government) made Hitler a **dictator**. This meant he had complete power. He could pass whatever laws he liked.

Jews forced out!

Under the **Nazis**, Jewish people were not allowed to mix with other Germans. They lost their jobs and had to sell their businesses. In November 1938 the Nazis destroyed thousands of Jewish shops and

These boys are from the Hitler Youth Movement. German boys between the ages of fourteen and eighteen joined the movement to learn Nazi ideas.

Word Bank

rabbi   someone trained in Jewish law and a leader of Jewish worshippers

synagogues. This event is known as *Kristallnacht*. *Kristallnacht* means "The Night of Broken Glass."

Prisons

In 1933 the Nazis began setting up prisons called **concentration camps.** They sent Jews, gay people, **Roma** (gypsies), and anyone who disagreed with them to these camps. Also, the Nazis did not want to spend money on disabled people. Between October 1939 and August 1941, they killed more than 70,000 disabled people.

The inside of this synagogue was completely destroyed during *Kristallnacht*.

synagogue Jewish place of worship

Operation *Kindertransports*

After *Kristallnacht*, the British government allowed ten thousand Jewish children from Germany, Austria, and Czechoslovakia to move to Great Britain. But they had to go without their parents. This was known as Operation *Kindertransports*. *Kindertransports* means "transport for children."

A new life

In 1939 Lee Edwards left Germany at the age of fifteen. Her mother cried when they said good-bye. They never met again. Lee went to live with a Jewish family in England.

These are Jewish children from the first *Kindertransport*. They have just arrived in Harwich, England.

Word Bank   death camp   camp where the Nazis sent Jews and others to be killed

When she arrived, Lee found a pretty necklace in her suitcase. It was a last gift from her mother.

Sad news

After the war, Lee found out that her mother was dead. She had died in a **death camp**. Her father had killed himself.

Lee married and moved to the United States. She still remembers her mother. Her mother saved Lee's life by sending her away. Lee will always treasure her necklace.

Jewish children in the Holocaust

This is what happened to Jewish children in the **Holocaust**:

- Nearly 30,000 children survived in hiding.

- About 1.5 million children died.

A young Jewish-German girl arrives in England with her dolls.

Holocaust the killing of millions of Jews and other people by the Nazis

UNDER NAZI OCCUPATION

In 1939 Hitler's armies began invading other European countries. By 1941 the **Nazis** controlled a huge area of Europe.

Ghettos and labor camps

The Nazis forced all Jews to move to run-down parts of their towns. These areas were known as **ghettos**. The Nazis also set up **labor camps**. Jews were often worked to death in these camps. Many non-Jews were also sent to the ghettos and labor camps. They included the German **Roma** (gypsies).

Who are the Roma?

The Roma are sometimes called gypsies or Romanies. They are a traveling people. They have their own language and way of life. The Nazis hated the Roma. They tried to wipe out all of them.

Hitler inspects his soldiers. The year is 1939, and they have just invaded Poland.

A group of Roma at a labor camp in Poland, 1942.

Word Bank

ghetto   part of a town where Jewish people were forced to live. The Nazis built walls around ghettos and guarded their gates.

Death squads and deportation

When the Nazis invaded the **Soviet Union** in 1941, they set up **death squads**. Their job was to murder Jews in large numbers. The Nazis also began **deporting** Jews from the countries they occupied. The Nazis sent the Jews to ghettos and camps in Poland and Germany.

← German invasion in 1939
← German invasion in 1940
← German invasion in 1941

B   BELGIUM
N   NETHERLANDS
SWITZ   SWITZERLAND

0   500 km
0   400 miles

This is a map of Europe. It shows Germany's invasions up to 1941.

deport   force someone to move to another country

Irène's story

Irène Rusak and her family were Jews living in Belgium. In 1940 the **Nazis** invaded Belgium. Irène was thirteen years old. In 1942 the Nazis sent Irène's oldest sister to Auschwitz. She was killed in this camp.

Shelter in a convent

Irène's parents hid one of their remaining four daughters with a non-Jewish family. Then they found a **convent** that would take Irène and her two other sisters. They had to pretend to be Christians.

Irène in later life. She married and went to live in England.

Father Bruno with five Jewish children whom he sheltered.

The hidden children

Some Jewish children survived because their parents gave them to kind, non-Jewish people. A Belgian monk named Father Bruno helped hundreds of Jewish children. These children had to pretend to be Christians.

Word Bank   convent place where nuns live and work

Anne Frank in hiding

Anne Frank and her family were German Jews. In 1933 they moved to the Netherlands. But in 1940 the Nazis invaded their new country.

The hiding place

Anne's family hid in secret rooms above her father's office. They had to stay hidden and quiet at all times. Sadly, the Nazis discovered the family. They sent them to Auschwitz. Anne was just thirteen. Only her father survived the camp.

"When I think about our lives here, I usually think that we live in a paradise compared to the Jews who aren't in hiding."

An extract from Anne Frank's diary.

Anne Frank (third from right) walks next to her father in happier days.

Arek Hersh

Arek Hersh was sent to a **labor camp** in Poland. He was eleven years old. The prisoners had to work for fourteen hours a day. Many of them tried to kill themselves. The **Nazis** murdered prisoners for breaking the rules.

Dying of hunger

The prisoners in the camp were always hungry. Each day they had only one small piece of bread, some black coffee, and a little soup. Some people died of hunger.

Polish men, and boys of Arek's age, were sent to work in labor camps.

Word Bank   labor camp   prison where Jews and others were sent to work for the Nazis

As time went on, there was less food, and the prisoners had to work harder. The camp started with 2,500 men. Eighteen months later, only eleven were still alive. Arek was one of them. He was sent to several other camps, and finally to Auschwitz.

After the war

Arek survived the war and went to England. He was the only member of his family left alive. The eighty other members of his family had all died in the **Holocaust**.

Prisoners make clothes at Sachsenhausen **concentration camp** in Germany. The year is 1941.

prisoner of war (POW)   prisoner who is captured and put in prison by the enemy during a war

LIFE IN THE GHETTOS

Secret photos

The Nazis did not allow Jewish people to take photos. But Zvi Kadushin took photos secretly. He took some outdoor photos through a buttonhole in his coat. Zvi took the photo below in 1941. It shows the Kovno ghetto in Poland.

In 1939 the **Nazis** forced Jews to live in **ghettos**. The ghettos were areas in poor parts of towns. The Nazis built walls around the ghettos. They also put armed guards at the gates to stop the Jews from escaping.

The Nazis crammed huge numbers of people into these ghettos. Whole families lived in one room. There was little work for them and little to eat.

The Nazis chose groups of Jewish people to form **Jewish Councils**. These councils had to follow Nazi

Word Bank Nazis people in the political party that ran Germany from 1933 to 1945

orders and run the ghettos. Anyone who didn't do his or her job was killed.

Surviving the ghettos

Jewish people did their best to survive. The people helped each other. They ran schools and put on concerts. But life was hard. Many died of hunger and disease. It was hard to get medicine.

The Nazis did not allow schools in the ghettos. This picture shows a secret school in the Lodz ghetto, Poland.

The market in the Warsaw ghetto, Poland, in 1941. People came here to exchange the few goods they had. Between July and December 1941, almost 30,000 Jews died of starvation in Warsaw.

ghetto   part of a town where Jewish people were forced to live. The Nazis built walls around ghettos and guarded their gates.

Victor Breitburg and the Lodz ghetto

Victor Breitburg arrived in the Lodz **ghetto** in Poland in 1941. He was fourteen years old. He lived in one small room with his parents, his sister, and his brother. People in the ghetto were starving.

Victor was lucky. He had a job in a woodwork factory. Because of this, he received extra food.

Taken away

In September 1942 the **Nazis** took away all the patients from the ghetto hospital. They also **deported** 25,000 Jews under 10 and over 65 years old. But Victor and his father found a tunnel. They hid seventeen children and their mothers in the tunnel.

The Lodz ghetto

The Lodz ghetto was in Poland. It was one of the largest ghettos set up by the Nazis. Nearly 230,000 Jewish people lived in it. The ghetto was set up in February 1940. In 1942 people in Lodz ghetto were deported to **concentration camps**. In 1944 those remaining in the ghetto were deported and killed.

This picture was taken in the Lodz ghetto in 1942. All Jewish people had to wear a yellow **Star of David** like the star this man is wearing.

Word Bank   deport   force someone to move to another country

Auschwitz survivor

In June 1944 Victor's family was sent to Auschwitz-Birkenau. Victor was selected to work in Auschwitz. He survived the war. The rest of his family was murdered.

Jewish photographer Mendel Grossman took photos secretly in the Lodz ghetto. Here, a boy feeds his little sister. Many people starved to death in the ghettos.

Star of David   star-shaped symbol of Jewish identity

The murder plan

In January 1942 the **Nazis** held a special meeting. This meeting became known as the Wannsee Conference. At the meeting, the Nazis decided on a way to get rid of the Jews forever. They called this plan the "Final Solution."

Off to the camps

The Nazis emptied the **ghettos**. They sent the healthiest Jews to **labor camps** in Poland. These people had to work there

These Jews are leaving Westerbork camp in the Netherlands. They are being sent by train to Auschwitz in 1942.

Word Bank   Allied belonging to the countries that fought together against the Nazis

until they died from hunger, illness, or exhaustion. Everyone else went to **death camps**. In the death camps, the Jews were killed.

Few survivors

By 1944 the Nazis had closed all the ghettos. Almost all the Jews had gone to death camps. Only a few survived until the end of the war. They were freed by Soviet and other **Allied** forces.

Heinrich Himmler (1900–1945)

Heinrich Himmler was the second most powerful Nazi, after Hitler. In 1941 he took control of the **death squads**. These squads killed about half a million Jews in Eastern Europe. In December 1941 he took control of the death camps in Poland.

Himmler (in the car) talks to a Jew in the Lodz ghetto. Himmler visited the ghetto in 1942.

death camp camp where the Nazis sent Jews and others to be killed

Many people were dying in **concentration camps** and **labor camps**. But the **Nazis** wanted to find a quick way of killing the Jews.

In 1941 they set up **death camps** in Poland. The Nazis could kill large numbers of people at a time in these camps.

Oskar Schindler

Oskar Schindler (second from left in the picture above) was a German businessman. He ran a factory in Poland using Jewish workers. Schindler **bribed** the Nazis to save his workers from the labor camps. He saved about one thousand Jewish lives.

Gas chambers

People arrived at a death camp and went straight to the **gas chambers**. The Nazis said that the chambers

This is one of the gas chambers at Auschwitz.

Word Bank   gas chamber   room used by the Nazis to gas people to death

were showers. But when the people were inside, the guards turned on poison gas. The people choked to death. Then their bodies were burned in large ovens.

Terrible tasks

A few Jews were saved to do horrible jobs. They had to clean out the ovens or sort through the dead people's belongings. Between December 1941 and October 1943, the Nazis murdered at least two million Jews in Polish death camps.

The Nazis treated their prisoners like animals. These men are being forced to pull a trailer.

bribe give someone something, such as money, to persuade them to behave in a certain way

Max Perkal

Max Perkal was born in Poland in 1926. In 1941 Max and his family had to move to a Jewish **ghetto**. In 1943 the **Nazis** sent the family to Auschwitz.

Max was now seventeen. At Auschwitz, he was put to work. Max saw people go to the **gas chambers**. He also saw their bodies after they had been gassed.

Working for the enemy

In December 1943, Max started work in a factory at Auschwitz. He made weapons. He had to work

These Hungarian Jews are arriving at Auschwitz in 1944. Very soon after this photo was taken, most of these people were killed. ➜

Word Bank

ghetto part of a town where Jewish people were forced to live. The Nazis built walls around ghettos and guarded their gates.

for twelve hours a day. Max survived more than a year at the factory.

Free at last

In January 1945 the Nazis closed Auschwitz. They moved Max to Buchenwald **concentration camp**. Three months later, U.S. soldiers freed him.

Max went to live in the United States. He was the only member of his family to survive the **Holocaust**.

Survival of twins

Eva Mozes Kor is shown below holding a picture of herself and her twin sister. The twins were sent to Auschwitz concentration camp. Most children were killed, but the Nazis conducted terrible medical experiments on twins. Luckily, both girls survived.

Holocaust the killing of millions of Jews and others by the Nazis

Kitty Hart

Kitty Hart was a Jewish girl from Poland. The **Nazis** did not know Kitty and her mother were Jews. When Kitty was fourteen, she and her mother were sent to Germany. Like many other Polish people, they became slave workers in a factory.

Then somebody told the Nazis that Kitty and her mother were Jews. They were both sent to Auschwitz **labor camp**.

This woman was forced to work in a German factory making weapons.

Prisoners in the Belsen **concentration camp** became horribly thin.

How did some people survive?

Some prisoners survived because they were useful in running the camp. They included doctors, nurses, dentists, and musicians. These people were given extra food.

Word Bank   labor camp   prison where Jews and others were sent to work for the Germans

Basic essentials

Each prisoner had a bowl. It was used both as a food bowl and a toilet. The prisoners had nowhere to wash either themselves or the bowl.

Horrible jobs

Kitty had to work in the nearby Birkenau **death camp**. She sorted the belongings of the dead people. She scooped up human waste. Kitty and her mother survived twenty months in Auschwitz. Kitty was seventeen when Americans freed them from a camp in Germany.

Life in Auschwitz

Kitty Hart survived Auschwitz, but life was hard:

"I saw myself as a fox, avoiding the hunters. If you're afraid, you must creep away. You mustn't fight."

A prisoner sorts through gold rings taken from prisoners in Buchenwald concentration camp.

death camp   camp where the Nazis sent Jews and others to be killed

RESISTANCE!

A few countries refused **Nazi** orders to send Jews to their deaths. In 1943 the Nazis ordered Finland and Bulgaria to **deport** their Jews. These orders caused huge **protests** in both countries. As a result, Finnish and Bulgarian Jews were not deported.

Other people also protected the Jews from the Nazis. In Denmark, sailors shipped most of the Danish Jews to safety in Sweden. This way, the Nazis could not deport them. In some countries, brave people hid Jews from the Nazis.

These Soviet partisans in 1943 are taking a break before their next battle with the Nazis.

Word Bank

rebellion when a group of people join together to fight against the people who are in power

Fighting and rebelling

In countries such as France, Poland, and the **Soviet Union**, people formed **partisan** groups. These were armed groups that fought the Nazis. The groups also sheltered Jews who escaped from the Nazis. Many escaped Jews formed armed groups of their own.

Sometimes, people in the ghettos **rebelled** against the Nazis in the **ghettos**. There were even **rebellions** in the **death camps** and **labor camps**.

These German soldiers are taking photographs of a dead Soviet man in 1942. The Nazis killed the man.

Punished for fighting back

The Nazis killed those who fought them. They also punished their communities. In January 1943 Mendel Fiszlewicz attacked a German commander in Poland. The Nazis killed him. Then they shot 25 men and sent 300 women and children to Treblinka death camp.

---

partisan   person who was part of an armed group set up to fight the Nazis

Vitka Kempner

Vitka Kempner grew up in Kalish, Poland. When Vitka was nineteen, the Germans invaded Kalish. They sent the Jews to a **monastery**. Vitka escaped. She went to Vilna (now part of Lithuania).

A daring plan

In 1941 the **Nazis** occupied Vilna. Some Jews formed a secret organization to fight the Nazis. Vitka joined them. In 1943 Vitka's group carried out a daring attack on the Nazis. They blew up the

Jewish fighters

Between 20,000 and 30,000 Jews formed **partisan** groups to fight the Nazis. These Jews had escaped from ghettos and **labor camps**. They destroyed thousands of German trains, power plants, and factories.

Soviet fighters make sure their weapons are clean and ready for action.

Word Bank   monastery   place where monks live and pray

railroad and damaged a German train carrying military equipment.

The end of the ghetto

In September 1943 the Nazis destroyed the Vilna **ghetto**. The fighters from the ghetto escaped through the sewers. Vitka and some of the other Jewish fighters began living in the forest. They continued fighting the Nazis.

Vitka survived the **Holocaust**. She married Jewish fighter, Abba Kovner. They moved to **Palestine**.

A way to die
Jewish fighter Abba Kovner described the choice that Jewish people faced:
"If we are cowards, we die. If we are brave, we die. So we might as well act bravely."

These partisans are laying explosives on a railroad line around Kursk in the **Soviet Union**. There were huge battles between the German and Soviet forces in 1943.

Palestine territory in the Middle East by the Mediterranean Sea that was divided when Israel was formed in 1948

Marek Edelman

Marek Edelman was a Polish Jew born in 1921. He grew up in Warsaw, Poland. The **Nazis** occupied Warsaw in 1939. In 1940 they forced all the Jews into the Warsaw **ghetto**.

The Jewish Fighting Organization

From July to September 1942, the Nazis sent about 300,000 Jews from the Warsaw ghetto to Treblinka **death camp**. Marek and some other young people set up the Jewish Fighting Organization.

Call for action

A call from the Jewish Fighting Organization in the fall of 1942:

"Jewish people, the time has come. You must be prepared to resist. Not a single Jew should go to the railroad cars. If you can't fight, go into hiding."

Fighters in the Warsaw ghetto prepare for action. Thousands of people in the ghetto joined the Jewish Fighting Organization to **resist** the Nazis.

Word Bank   resist fight back and refuse to do as you are told

Battle for the ghetto

On April 19, 1943, the Nazis returned to the ghetto. The Jewish fighters had guns. Marek led one of four groups of fighters. They fired on the Nazis.

The Nazis began to burn all the buildings in the ghetto. By May 16 they had destroyed the ghetto. Seven thousand Jews died. About 50,000 were sent to death camps and **concentration camps**.

Marek escaped through the sewers. He kept working against the Nazis and survived the war.

The Warsaw ghetto during the uprising in 1943. The Nazis burned down buildings to stop the **resistance**.

World War II ends

In late 1942 the **Nazis** began to lose the war. Early in 1945 **Allied** soldiers freed the few prisoners still alive in the camps. The war in Europe finally ended in May 1945.

The troops who first entered the camps were sickened by what they saw. The survivors were horribly thin. They looked like living skeletons. Dead bodies lay everywhere.

U.S. soldiers in Buchenwald **concentration camp,** just after they freed it in April 1945. The soldiers came too late for the dead prisoners in this trailer. ➡

Word Bank   **Allied** belonging to the countries that fought together against the Nazis

The survivors

About two-thirds of Europe's Jews died in the **Holocaust**. Very few prisoners survived the camps. Many of those survivors felt guilty and ashamed to be still alive. Some killed themselves.

After the war, Jewish survivors went back to their home countries or moved abroad. About 40,000 moved to the United States and about 83,000 moved to **Palestine**. In 1948 the Jewish state of Israel was formed there.

The Nuremberg Trials

In 1945–1946 some leading Nazis were put on trial in Nuremberg, Germany. Twelve of those found guilty were put to death. Many Nazis escaped trial. Shown below on trial are Hermann Goering (A), commander-in-chief of the German air force, and Rudolph Hess (B), Hitler's deputy before the war.

Holocaust the killing of millions of Jews and others by the Nazis

Bella Azar

Bella Azar was born in Iasi, Romania, in 1932. In 1941 thousands of Jews in Iasi were robbed, beaten, and killed. A German officer beat up nine-year-old Bella in the street.

In the orphanage

In 1942 Bella's mother placed Bella and her sister in an **orphanage** for safety. The children had to work hard there, but they survived the **Holocaust**.

The parents of these Jewish children all died in **concentration camps**. The children are being sent to live with the Jewish community in **Palestine**.

Word Bank   kibbutz (plural **kibbutzim**)   community set up by some Jewish people who settled in Palestine

Moving to Israel

In 1947 a Jewish organization took a group of children to Haifa in Israel. Bella and Esther went as part of this group. At Haifa, the children were divided into different age groups. They were sent to live in communities called **kibbutzim**.

A wonderful surprise

As Bella was getting on a truck to go to her new home, an old woman came up. She asked Bella if she was from Iasi and if she knew Bella and Esther. The woman was her own mother. They had not recognized each other. It was an amazing moment.

Israel time line

After the war, many Jews moved to Palestine. They established the country of Israel there.

1917—Britain takes over Palestine.

1936–1939—Palestinian Arabs fight against British rule.

1947—The **United Nations** plans to divide Palestine between the Jews and Palestinians.

1948—Jews establish the country of Israel in Palestine.

◄ This photo shows Israel's first prime minister, David Ben-Gurion, on May 14, 1948. He is declaring the establishment of the state of Israel.

United Nations organization made up of many countries. It tries to solve world problems in a peaceful way.

Primo Levi

Primo Levi was born in Italy in 1919. When he grew up, he became a chemist. The **Nazis** invaded Italy in 1943. Primo fought against the Germans. He was caught in 1944 and sent to Auschwitz. He was useful to the Germans because he was a chemist. He worked in a factory near Auschwitz.

Primo's luck

Just when the Germans emptied Auschwitz camp, Primo became very ill. This turned out to be lucky for him. The Nazis thought he was dead

The Italian writer Primo Levi. His books remain popular today. His writing reminds people in a very moving way about the terrible events of the **Holocaust**.

A guide talks to students at a Holocaust memorial. This memorial is in Miami Beach, Florida.

Word Bank   civilian   person who is not in the armed forces

and left him behind. In January 1945 Soviet soldiers liberated the camp, and he was freed.

Guilt and shame

Primo became a writer. He published his last book in 1986. In the book, he wrote about the guilt he felt. He had survived when most Jews did not. He felt he was living in the place of those who had died. Primo was **depressed** for a long time. Finally, in 1987 he killed himself.

These Jewish children survived Buchenwald **concentration camp**. They are making the Jewish symbol of the **Star of David**.

Roma (gypsies) people who travel around to live and work

1919 The National Socialist German Workers' Party, also known as the **Nazi** Party, is set up.

1921 Adolf Hitler becomes leader of the Nazi Party.

1932 The Nazis become the most popular party in Germany.

1933 Hitler becomes the ruler of Germany. **Concentration camps** are set up.

1935 New laws take away the rights of German Jews.

1938 Germany takes over Austria and part of Czechoslovakia.
The Nazis attack Jews in Germany and Austria during *Kristallnacht*.
Jewish children are taken to Britain on the *Kindertransports*.

1939 Germany invades the rest of Czechoslovakia and Poland.
World War II begins.
The Nazis set up **ghettos** for Jews.

1940 German armies conquer Denmark, Norway, Belgium, the Netherlands, Luxembourg, and France.

1941 Germany invades Yugoslavia, Greece, and the **Soviet Union**.
Death squads are set up.
The first **death camps** are set up.

1942 The Nazis hold the Wannsee Conference. They agree on a plan to kill all the Jews in Europe in an organized way.
More death camps are set up.

1943   People in the Warsaw ghetto rise up against the Nazis.
Heinrich Himmler orders the closing of the ghettos.
People in the Vilna ghetto rise up against the Nazis.

1944
January Soviet troops start to move into Poland.
June   **Allied** forces enter Rome, Italy.
Allied troops land in Normandy, France (D-Day).
July   Soviet forces free prisoners in Majdanek death camp in Poland.
August   The **Allies** free Paris, France.
Soviet troops take Bucharest, Romania.
October The Allies free Athens, Greece.
Germans surrender at Aachen, in Germany.
The **gas chambers** are used for the last time at Auschwitz.

1945   Allied and Soviet troops free the surviving prisoners in the camps.
May   Germany surrenders.

1945–46 Some leading Nazis are put on trial. Some are put to death or imprisoned.

1948   The state of Israel is set up.

Organizations

United States Holocaust Memorial Museum
This museum is a national memorial to those who died in the Holocaust. It aims to educate people about the Holocaust with film, photos, objects, documents, and eyewitness accounts. There is a special exhibition for children and a computer-based learning center.
The museum runs educational programs and traveling exhibitions. You can contact the museum at the following address:
100 Raoul Wallenberg Place, SW
Washington, DC
20024-2126

Books

Abells, Chana Byers. *The Children We Remember.* New York: Harper Trophy, 2002.

Lawton, Clive A. *Auschwitz. The Story of a Nazi Death Camp*. Cambridge, Mass.: Candlewick, 2002.

Poole, Josephine. *Anne Frank*. New York: Knopf Books for Young Readers, 2005.

Zullo, Allan and Mara Bovsun. *Survivors: True Stories of Children in the Holocaust*. New York: Scholastic, 2005.

DVD/VHS

Films about the Holocaust often contain information and scenes that can be deeply distressing. Ask a parent or teacher about such films before watching any of them.

Yellow Star—The Persecution of the Jews in Europe 1933–1945 (VHS, 1997)
A documentary that looks at the treatment of the Jews in Europe while Hitler was in power.

World Wide Web

To find out more about the Holocaust you can search the Internet. Use keywords such as these:
- "Warsaw ghetto"
- World War II + Jews
- "Jewish Fighting Organization"

You can find your own keywords by using words from this book. The search tips below will help you find useful Web sites.

Most Web sites are aimed at adults. They can contain upsetting information and pictures. Beware! A few people believe that the Holocaust did not happen at all. They have Web sites that wrongly say they are giving the facts. Make sure that you use well-known sites with correct information.

Search tips

There are billions of pages on the Internet. It can be difficult to find exactly what you are looking for. These tips will help you find useful Web sites more quickly:
- Know what you want to find out about.
- Use simple keywords.
- Use two to six keywords in a search.
- Only use names of people, places, or things.
- Put quotation marks around words that go together, for example, "Vilna ghetto."

Where to search

Search engine
A search engine looks through millions of Web site pages. It lists all the sites that match the words in the search box. You will find the best matches are at the top of the list on the first page.

Search directory
A person instead of a computer has sorted a search directory. You can search by keyword or subject and browse through the different sites. It is like looking through books on a library shelf.

GLOSSARY

Allied belonging to the countries that fought together against the Nazis

Allies countries such as Britain, France, the Soviet Union, and the United States that fought against Nazi Germany

Aryans people from Germany and Scandinavia whom the Nazis thought were superior to everyone else

bribe give someone something, such as money, to persuade them to behave in a certain way

civilian person who is not in the armed forces

concentration camp prison where the Nazis sent their enemies to teach them to be Nazis. Many thousands died in these camps.

convent place where nuns live and work

death camp camp where the Nazis sent Jews and others to be killed

death squad group of Nazis whose job it was to shoot Jews

deport force someone to move to another country

depressed feeling extremely sad and unhappy

dictator ruler who has complete power over a country

gas chamber room used by the Nazis to gas people to death

ghetto part of a town where Jewish people were forced to live. The Nazis built walls around ghettos and guarded their gates.

Holocaust the killing of millions of Jews and others by the Nazis

Jewish Council group of Jewish people chosen to run a ghetto

kibbutz (plural **kibbutzim**) community set up by some Jewish people who settled in Palestine

labor camp prison where Jews and others were sent to work for the Nazis

monastery place where monks live and pray

Nazi member of the political party that ran Germany from 1933 to 1945

orphanage home for children with no parents to care for them

Palestine territory in the Middle East by the Mediterranean Sea that was divided when Israel was formed in 1948

partisan person who was part of an armed group set up to fight the Nazis

prisoner of war (POW) prisoner who is captured and put in prison by the enemy during a war

protest occasion when people show that they disagree with, or do not approve of, something

rabbi someone trained in Jewish law and a leader of Jewish worshippers

rebel fight against those who are in power, or a person who fights against those who are in power

rebellion when a group of people join together to fight against the people who are in power

resist fight back and refuse to do as you are told

resistance people fighting back and refusing to do what they are told

Roma (gypsies) people who travel around to live and work

Soviet Union country that once spread across northern Asia into Eastern Europe and included what is now Russia

Star of David star-shaped symbol of Jewish identity

synagogue Jewish place of worship

United Nations organization made up of many countries. It tries to solve world problems in a peaceful way.

INDEX